Listen:
http://thirdmanbooks.com/ericalewis
password: superwoman

Printed in Nashville, Tennessee.

Library of Congress Cataloging-in-Publication Data

Names: Lewis, Erica, author.
Title: Mary wants to be a superwoman / by Erica Lewis.
Description: First edition. | Nashville, Tennessee : Third Man Books, [2017]
Identifiers: LCCN 2016053328 | ISBN 9780996401616 (softcover)
Classification: LCC PS3612.E9645 A6 2017 | DDC 811/.6--dc23
LC record available at https://lccn.loc.gov/2016053328

FIRST EDITION
Book cover and layout design by Jessica Yohn.
Cover photo taken by erica lewis, "document 7" from the dead girl series.
All other photos taken from the Jelks/Lawton family archives.

mary wants to be a superwoman

erica lewis

these songs for us all,

erica xo

THIRD MAN BOOKS
NASHVILLE, TENNESSEE

Mary Wants to be a Superwoman

You can hear happiness
Staggering on
Down the street
Footprints dressed in red
And the wind screams Mary

— The Jimi Hendrix Experience, *The Wind Cries Mary*

I want to learn to sing
I want to learn to sing with emotion and intelligence

— Paige Taggart, *Want for Lion*

I sing because I'm happy
I sing because I'm free
For His eye is on the sparrow
And I know He watches me

— Civilla D. Martin and Charles H. Gabriel (1905), *His Eye Is on the Sparrow*

project note

mary wants to be a superwoman is the second book in the box set trilogy.

Like *daryl hall is my boyfriend*, the first book in the trilogy, *mary wants to be a superwoman* uses the music of a (once popular) pop artist that I grew up listening to. Each poem takes its title from a line of a Stevie Wonder song—the poems are not "about" the actual songs, but what is triggered when listening to or thinking about the music. I'm thinking about what happens when you take something like a pop song and turn it in on itself, give it a different frame of reference, juxtapose the work against itself, against other pop music, and bring it into the present.

While the entire project is my take on revising the confessional, the poems from *mary wants to be a superwoman* delve more into my family history, specifically the women on my mother's side and their voices within that history, and also take inspiration from a list of female poets and friends. My family history is complicated like any family history in America. *mary* is all about processing that history, the day to day, dealing with a history that has been passed down, to an extent, stories and memories that I had nothing to do with, and how to live and move on from that history and its implications.

for
the jelks women
the lawton women

and for my friends

contents

introduction *by tyrone williams*

"But does she really know what's in her head"? If the first line of Stevie Wonder's 1972 eight-minute suite from his debut solo album applies to her mother, Mary Lewis-Jelks, a black woman inculcated with a formidable will to survive that would serve as the foundation for the figure of the stereotypical "black matriarch," summarized in Daniel Patrick Moynihan's influential 1965 report, *The Negro Family: The Case for National Action*, the second line, which begins this essay, might well describe the erica lewis of this book and its predecessor, *daryl hall is my boyfriend*. The significance of that Stevie Wonder lyric is not so much what it says about "mary" but what it says about the speaker, presuming to know "mary" better than she knows herself. Both sides of that lyric—what the speaker thinks "mary" thinks, what "mary" thinks—might well explain the multiple layers of interrogation (self, family, friends, etc.) lewis deploys in *mary wants to be a superwoman*.

Following Ralph Ellison's distinction between ancestors (aesthetic kin) and relatives (blood relations), one might say that erica lewis, granddaughter of O'Hara, Koch and the New York School as well as granddaughter of Ginsberg, Kerouac, Kaufman and the other Beats, is part of the second generation of poets born in the wake of the Civil Rights Movement and the first generation of poets born at the birth of Language Writing. Her aesthetic filiations crisscross any number of tendencies and movements in postmodernist and contemporary American poetry. She counts among her sisters and brothers Gina Myers, Brenda Iijima, Michelle Detorie, ΩSampson Starkweather and Dana Ward. As I will explain below, these are her sisters and brothers—and not just friends—in the black power sense of the terms, shared allegiances to overlapping social, cultural and aesthetic values. In deleting what was deemed the most important criterion for being a sister or brother—racial authenticity—I am following lewis' lead: she is no less (and no more) the daughter of Language Writing (and other poetry movements) than she is the daughter of Ms. Lewis-Jelks.

Like so many young poets of her generation, erica lewis has absorbed the lessons of the generations of artists who wrote under the Cold War and post-*glasnost/perestroika* era as well as the lessons of her contemporaries writing under the clouds of interminable internal and external wars. In both cases, historical and contemporary, the wars were and are internal (e.g., the Civil Rights Movement and Black Lives Matter) and external (e.g., Vietnam and the 1991 and 2003 Gulf Wars). In this context, people like me, the first *generation* of Black Americans expected to attend college, drink from public water fountains and eat at restaurants unencumbered by *de jure*, if not *de facto*, segregation and racial discrimination, wore the capes, were burdened with the capes (whether we wanted them or not), of super—if not great—expectations. However, like my parents, lewis' parents are part of that transitional generation that lived and worked both before and after the passage of the various Civil Rights bills. Their sense of dislocation (e.g., the second Great Migration from the South to the North) and ambivalence (e.g., the integration of public schools cost many black educators working in all black schools their jobs) is not mine, and mine are not erica lewis', but she has inherited her own sense of dislocation and ambivalence, personal and general, and both mark *mary wants to be a superwoman*. That first line of the Stevie Wonder song that titles this transitional book of poetry—it is the second in a projected trilogy—marks the ambivalence, if not outright hostility, a mid-20th century black man may have felt about a mid-20th century black woman not satisfied to imitate the domestic life of white housewives extolled and idealized in those 1950s and 1960s soap ads. Elaine Brown and Michelle Wallace, just to name two, have written about the ways that a resurgent black patriarchy accompanied, indeed, drove, the marches, peaceful and not, civil and militant, toward the horizon of black liberation and black power. In this tribute to her mother and, by extension, the other women in her family (see the poem "i lived to see the milk and honey land"), lewis shuffles back and forth between her parents' generation and her own, exploring the constellation of her identities—artist, publicist, friend, spouse and daughter. Thus these poems are marked by her aesthetic and sanguineous inheritances. A propagator of the new lyric, New Narrative and Language Writing, erica lewis is part African American, part Cherokee and part white.

Does this miscellany of genetic and aesthetic influences free poets like lewis to explore the terrains of American social and cultural fields unfettered by preconceptions (e.g., racial or aesthetic) or is it, in fact, a burden inasmuch as there's no escaping social, cultural and, yes, racial preconceptions? Are her peers just her sisters and brothers or are they, too, writing under great expectations (their own or others) as supersisters and superbrothers? Can I really draw analogies between their aesthetic, political and social struggles and those of the baby boomer generation framing the "short" Civil Rights Movement (1955-1968)? If I insist on the analogies it's because no one, black or white, born in the 20th or 21st century can escape the domino effects of our shared national history, and by that I mean not only the social, economic and political spheres but also the cultural and, more narrowly, the aesthetic spheres. As the inheritors of various modernist, postmodernist, neo-modernist (e.g., Language Writing) and neo-postmodernist (e.g., Flarf) movements in poetry and poetics, the current mature generation (by which I mean those between their mid-thirties and mid-forties) of poets have before them a plethora of aesthetic models. Thanks to the proliferation of writing programs, the internet and desktop publishing, this generation has, as it were, no excuse for not mastering the poetry traditions and anti-traditions so widely available thanks to the internet. But of course these are also the problems—the traditions and anti-traditions. Opportunities and crises as tradition and anti-tradition. The democratization of publishing techniques and platforms, the erasure of the bar between the "minor" and "major" leagues in terms of presses, means that poets who have not yet published a book, who still think of the book as the standard for legitimacy, have fewer excuses on which to fall. More important than this admittedly exaggerated state, the "rewards" have also flattened out: both inside and outside the "po' biz," a book that gets great reviews and/or prizes will have as much a general impact as books engulfed in the silence of perceived irrelevance. Poets are thus enjoined (perhaps from within as much as from without) to be superpoets. On this view the po' biz can be likened to a junkie that has to have an increasing quantity of dope to get the "same" high attained with that first hit. lewis' poetry betrays some of the uncertainty and unrest associated with this state of poetry. And that makes it a compelling barometer of the current state of things. That said, the particular inflection she brings to the poise of effortlessness—an attitude, if not quite an aesthetic, currently in vogue—as a black Native American white poet is as unsettling as it is compelling.

Like the first book in the trilogy, *daryl hall is my boyfriend*, *mary wants to be a superwoman* is a paean to the personal and national past, a kind of middle-age crisis work, though the crisis is sometimes well hidden beneath the casual, sharp, ragged (blunt) edges of lewis' writing. Each poem in the book is framed by phrases from the lyrics of Stevie Wonder's Motown records, from the early singles-oriented collections to the later, pioneering solo concept albums. The poems shuttle back and forth between the past and present, memory and perception, recollection and observation. The dominant theme and strategy is lewis' homages to her friends, often other contemporary women poets, and her homages to her women kin. And the dominant motif is brokenness, a word which appears, in its various noun and adjectival forms, eighteen times in the book. Although this motif does not always signal the separation of that which should be whole, separation, fragmentation and discontinuity are all over these poems. lewis responds to this motif of literal incoherence variously. Sometimes she's defiant ("fuck art, let's dance"), sometimes inspirational ("you fell down to the music / now get on up"), and sometimes resigned ("i got indian / blood in me / you can't heal / a wound / with logic"). A line like the last one might make one wonder if erica lewis also wants, or better still, needs to be a superwoman, everything to everyone, just like Mary Lewis-Jelks. Or can she simply be erica lewis? I suspect that family and national history say otherwise.

That doesn't mean lewis doesn't try to be "just" herself. Nor does it mean that she doesn't want to be "more" than just herself: "i want to be like patti smith, but with a little d'angelo / like a spiritual sibling." (23) The desire for transformation into someone other than herself, into someone "like" her heroines and heroes (it's important to note the similes in those lines), is doubtless related to a major source of ambivalence in the book: her blood family. After announcing that she's always wanted "to be a rock star / some kind of psychedelic neo-hippie vixen," lewis' persona declares that, "family secrets are the worst / so many things i've found out / over this last year / about people and history and our expectations / of people and history." (27) The tension between her supersisters and superbrothers and her family is formalized; the poems are mostly dedicated to her "chosen" family of peers but the subject matter is often lewis' conflicted relation to herself ("i am not as strong / as i pretend to be") and her blood family. This leads to a general criticism of racial authenticity and its familial roots in the second half of the book. In this context, to be "broken' is both personally painful ("i always feel / i am about to die / broken people jesus" and "we pour liquor / to appease / the slain / over the side / of some / stolen boat / broken body") and, per the diaspora, generally liberating ("there ain't no boat / there ain't no train / to take us back / the way / we came"). And lewis' attitude toward the presumption of solidarity on the basis of race and blood is perhaps best expressed in the middle of this book: "i just keep thinking / about this notion / of blackness / and how / we're supposed to dance." (62) lewis' criticism is not gratuitous; she goes on to delineate the false promises solidarity allegedly fulfills: "exceptionalism / and respectability / have never saved us / we are both / prisoner / and privileged / with both / our hands / on both sides / of the divide / we break down / so easily / into tribes…" (76) At the same time she rejects the conflation of blackness with long-suffering stoicism, precisely the stance underlying the so-called black matriarch: "you ain't black just because / you're numb to shit blowing up." (101)

And then there are the compromises of personal relationships, though in many of these poems lewis' lines function on multiple levels simultaneously. For example, these lines from the poem titled "when i needed you last winter" (a line from the Stevie Wonder song) can be read on the collective, familial and personal levels: "i mean i don't mind / that we, too / are almost always / the absence / of shared experience." (52) These lines register the persistent gaps (economic, social, cultural, etc.) between African Americans

4

and white Americans, between lewis and her family and perhaps between lewis and her partner. The default "exceptionalism" implied on so many levels here, read in conjunction with the lines in the previous paragraph regarding the exceptional, suggest that the dream of "shared experience" too often remains just that, a dream. Nonetheless, it is not insignificant that lewis refuses to give this state of things a positive valence, that her writing struggles to overcome division, that it, like she, fights to come in, as it were, from the cold. On her own terms, of course.

mary wants to be a superwoman is a book that tightropes the thin filament between, to use a musical metaphor, crossover potential and authentic blackness, to say nothing of its Cherokee undertones. In that respect this is a fugitive collection of poems, darting here and there, steps ahead of those who would attempt to locate its position by triangulation. Broken, wounded, erica lewis remains on the run, and as she writes, "all of my favorite people are broken." (99)

the wind screams mary

*clap your hands just a little bit louder**   *for mary lewis-jelks*

let me be home soon

in my fantasy i can't ever change

it was a past life thing, a past life thing

i am the child i am imagining

the present is still tenuous

porous modern life sprayed onto the wall

we're in a period of massive transformation

right now

i just want to comment on

that spiraling to something bigger

is there something bigger

i don't know

if we're there yet

i can't really move

pretty people believe too much

and for a split second everything in this room

becomes everything

i can't remember how the past felt

like what happened

to our familiars

let the ocean take me

the vertigo years

i've been praying for you

you get used to a place and don't notice things anymore

some part of you is fooled

but we are the reason

for one another

all of our spit and our bling

old blues to cover a new blues

gratitude and dislocation

the notion of place

as passage and return

i love you like we're in the movies

something gossamer that goes

straight through you

here are some more options

pain is a means of achieving perspective

not an end unto itself

like a film shot out of sequence

in high-spirited, even disorienting ways

and that says something for the indestructibility of love

the people you love and are loved by

a finitude that is anything but final

a little glitter

the new black

* "fingertips pts. 1 & 2"

i was thinking about writing's shifting place

in the hierarchy of needs for me

right now

i love me some home

the radio playing that forgotten song

deep drums

the kind that start storms

& it is like the best fairytale

once patterns become stationary and you absorb the distance

all blood tastes the same

in dusty rural americana

worth is actually kind of the perfect word

sent from my iphone

until the scars we collect reverse the flow

these are the words we use

and i am not sorry

to say goodbye

i need to be okay with loss

to think about all the times in my past

that i have lost something or given up

how those experiences have enriched me

like a sound that lands halfway between

oh goddamn yeah

i hate that i'm good at the things i don't care about

everything we see coming in

from the space around us

two hundred billion stars in our galaxy

the motions of our body

and life running for the train

like a little bitch

as the west coast burns, i listen to this song

which somehow reminds me of you

we lie under the trees and pray

for midwestern thunderstorms

sit down and look through the book

of botony sketches and feathers

we all try to learn

without sacrificing some purer sense of ourselves

but i'm no sailor

in my heart of hearts

i hope that you are too

it is the year of growing up

sweet mama time

the ease of selfhood and genuine soul

i'm fine thanks for asking

i'm an iron man

awakened by the clapping

✪ "uptight (everything's alright)"

you go north before you die

i've come to hate myself

today like it was yesterday

i was thinking about autobiography

the meaning of flesh and culture

bedroom pop daydreams

the expensive shit

life after life

the emeraude

the sharecropper

the sharecropper's son

how we don't show love until

we want love

in reality our most serious commitments

break us

as surely as they make us

what are we besides agreements

is that that kmart shit?

100,000 miles logged between the lessons

my desk is neatly organized

folders are clearly named

one day we will all be dead

behind the black and white

jesus i'm drunk on this

terrified of drowning in the gray

to invest in a person

is to acknowledge that they may fall apart

cured by falling snow

or rain or once

forgiveness sustains us all in advance

i stepped on a sign that said

be grateful

and now this is my dream

to let us be undone

gilding these sentiments with joy and awe

may all such clouds repair us

the unions we dare to call eternal

don't you ever wonder why you're here

what's going to happen to you after you die

there is nothing spectacular about this

the gift of your depression

your songs of joy & your other songs presently

*my baby loves me, my baby needs me**   *for sampson starkweather*

my long poem was reborn today

there is no single joy like

what you believe in

love and friendship and conviction

against all odds

still inspires me

we're all broke and naïve and our hearts

are green (money isn't real, people

just poetry)

to all my birds

one day all the stars will burn out

and here you are

getting something back from someone you hardly know

tell me which gods and goddesses we are again

the color of grief

the white space of reflection

i was aphrodite in that shmatta

that good good old school shit

standing in a city i don't know anymore

with bodies that do not know

the labor and history and death

can hurt you because history does not go away

our desire lacks

a second summer of love

i will never have any children

i would only bear them and confuse them

i am not yet sure

what the important language of speaking to each other

would sound like

somebody let me know my name

we wash up on the shore

and the roof caves in

not because we forget

that space and time are folded and refolded

but because it is possible

to be alive without having a heartbeat

we beat the drum

slowly bore holes into the walls

to shimmer and simultaneously

cut deep wounds

gathered across oceans

we cry often and softly

fly birds, fly

i want this song

i like simple math

i'm sitting here reading about adolf hitler

people talk a lot about random acts of violence

but it's not random

they have a trajectory a path

a history that can be followed

that you can look back on

like raindrops

it just seems random

but from the point of view of the ground

the raindrop was heading in that direction the whole time

where it intersects with the target

the perspective of the thing that gets hit

the ability to develop scar tissue

i'd rather be broken than empty

*i sit and wait in vain**   *for lisa howe*

who would want to dwell on the quietly agonizing, drawn-out times

remember how the story goes

at the end of the rainbow there's a pot of gold

but i really enjoy forgetting

when i first come to a place, i notice all the little details

the way the sky looks

the way people walk

doorknobs

everything

we see back towards the flood

try not to hold on to what is gone

the bridge of memories

how we kill ourselves

stumbling onto blue notes that didn't exist before

what if to love and be loved isn't enough

the slow-burning arrangements

this is me making love to my demons

i suspect my children will not exist

i am so damn tired

of driving over these mountains and crying

the void has nothing to do with death

or how you want to live

if you lived here, you'd be home by now

blood as union

our little commons

all stripped down

there are many dead fathers, but mine

without a doubt, it's easier not to know someone

poems proclaim a finitude

you are the ceo of sleeping

waking up so fucking slow

in 1987 i saw a video of madonna

it was very nice

all don't let them handle you

and you better start praying

not wanting to do anything over

it's strange to be at the mercy

of a stranger again

the comfort

of the way the room has been

transformed

thinking about lament

no dainty songs here

sung in a girlishly high register

each long, quiet moment

a glass of whiskey in my hand

i feel blessed

to have their hearts and minds

it was the ohio river

tellin' us to get ready and go

*your sweetie pie your precious one**   *for sommer browning*

this is a gospel for who knows

it's like we're supposed to peter pan ourselves every day

sleep just doesn't come that easy

we will always have bad dreams

our griefs and karmic baggage

the kind of petulance i think we all suffer from

this is supposed to be a glittering world

but shit, i sent you the magic free version

i hope that we can recover

from all of the stupid things

i love how you are in a vestibule

everything that happens right now happens

from cali and that feels so weird to me

i feel like i kinda want it to be a secret

like bitcoin for your heart

i mean when you go back home and you feel like a different person there

this was never your calling

a heavy mist permeates from the humid dance floor

a lariat around your wits

you know bootsy played here like two weeks ago

and i didn't go

if i told this to my 20 year old self

she would think i was a sad sad adult person

well, i'm gonna channel diana vreeland and put on my turban

read this in the moonlight

and see what happens

tender glitter aching

an admittance of your fragility

our hearts are pounding

we lost patience with the lord

can't you just see that maybe

just maybe you were the ocean

fuck art, let's dance

*i'm gonna patch up every single little dream**   *for paige taggart*

this will be our forgiveness rock record

to be brought to experience

when the blizzard ends

they throw a fucking huge parade

and this year will be the year that we win

our private thorns

trying not to live in

other people's tricked out fantasies

the wishes of your past

a long time ago we were famous

now we lead this kind of teenage life

not thinking we could fall

or what to consider truly embarrassing

in my dreams we're still screaming

dancing in the overdub

running through the yard

here is the song version of you

the sun is too bright

but i want the fucking sunshine

i want a daughter while i'm still young

i want to hold her hand

and show her some kind of beauty

last night when i saw you

i think maybe i said this was tonight

the past makes me cry it seems so wonderful

i cry i cry all the time

i can't help feeling sorry for myself

come back home cured

cured but nuts

i feel i want to tell you something

but i forget what

suddenly i just love you

suddenly i seem to be popular and have groupies

when we get together with our various disabilities it is funny

we need to have tea or drinks soon

or hit da club in our fugly stripper shoes

i hope it's nice out where you are today

we didn't even manage to get

a solid piece of the rainbow

but it is here

a song on my phone

the cars passing by

something old and familiar

outside my window

you are truly fantastic

where light meets air

and meaning becomes

observed by greatness

i feel truly blessed to have met you

you are saving me

epic brass chainz 4eva!

*i ain't playin hard for nobody**   *for carrie hunter*

jesus is on that main line

i'm happy to oblige

to live in the avant garde

brevity is my goddamn life

our brittle bones weren't meant to fly, boo

and all those feelings

a showcase of empty meaning

and escapist dream pop

maybe i'm just one of those people

forever unprepared for the passing of time

the shit we do

the music at the start

our thickness

and desire lines

it may sound mystical and bullshitty to you

but suddenly a person like me testifies

switches over to some gospel

some fucking indian chief

trying to be a civil person

i have not been this person for a very long time

i want to be like patti smith, but with a little d'angelo

like a spiritual sibling

i know you like the funny the light hearted me

between saturday night juke and sunday morning church

to lay your head down in the grass

in summer's parallels

we've all seen the birds

the masks that we fear we cannot live without

the difficulties of today and tomorrow

dressing for a good death

we try to meet in dreams

with only the wind whispering

it does seem like we would have the best love

you'd let me sing, too

here together are our hearts

artists are eager to prove their pop sensibilities

but we gave our kids all our youth

and all our lies

we're not trying to do some in fashion blah blah blah

we're trying to create something

that is emotionally truthful

the way you were when you were born

nestled in my closet

faced with yourself

it's been pure hustle

spring has never ever felt this good

i am addicted and i keep thinking

that's what i'll wear to the party

move to that dance

say time is a little container

not a healer

i want to finish what's her face's book

and just be done with it

i have this intense need to be liked

to see the new ink

and anything else you think might help

right now i don't believe in real life

memory is not real life

it's just a fact of feeling lost

something fierce

my friends are really saving me right now

hummingbirds with a little aubrey beardsley

you don't need

all the things you buy

i'd love to cross over, pretty mama

but the water's way too high

i didn't pay you to come out here

i didn't pay you for no boat rides

dancing in the shallows of the river

we hold on

to the life we aspire to

trying not to grow old

hear my train a comin'

well that's just how we roll

with the lights on

and some adult beverages

excited to hang out

to have luxury problems

we are crossing the bridge into sf now

meet there or close

the way here or here's hoping

god loves you when you're beautiful

and you are too beautiful to be a poet

i don't really want to sit in my house alone

with all this awesome booty

drinking a bottle of rosé

slapping my tattoo to stop the itch

i wouldn't mind a little fucking

reading the art of the personal essay

being held accountable for my own actions

but somehow everything you do

will be used against you

you've got too much visible shit

to keep your friends close

and your enemies closer

i am so glad

someone so beautiful

exists at all

*pretty little one**   *for adam wülfmeyer*

i always wanted to be a rock star

some kind of psychedelic neo-hippie vixen

my fake name on my real self

we all need that great love

to feel the burn of the sun on my skin

literally glittering

when the water in my body

wants to rise up

feel it coming near

and i don't know why

feel it in my blood

like the night of my birth

like the twenty-eighth year

i'll give it to you honest

family secrets are the worst

so many things i've found out

over this last year

about people and history and our expectations

of people and history

i'm very unsettled about what i know

and what i don't know

like stars circle and then burn out

what you for real look like

oh, the blood is speaking

i just want to warm my blood

i have this good sick body to share

i said come on jimi just lead me

i got shit to do

i was a little late to the party on this one

we speak about apology about the world in which we live

the thing you want the most inside you

this happiness chance

but i can't control all the ways that i'm falling

my own salty desires

archives

piecing (weaving)

a life back together

a tangible formalism

like architecture is a vow

like never before

i wish this was my problem

where the river water meets the ocean water

because we're all in debt

& we're all in love

something inside flickers

a strip light

on that old train song

take care of me lord

until i get home

when we were dreaming＊   *for rachel reader*

i don't know maybe i am a goddamn genius

though i hate writing on fb

end of my youth thing

dealing with the end of my 30s

and what is that? the end of my older youth?

my real life

all brooding and bohemian

well, you are in my trilogy

and to be honest, i'm not dealing very well with anything

emotional cutting just to see

if i'm literally going numb

lips and toes and fingers

everything trying to escape

through the extremities

so this is bigger than us

we talk shit

expecting to change shit

the world the world the world

this goddamned georgia dream

i wish i was there for real

& the fear & the honesty & connections & sadness

i am telling you all of this

all of these are tonight's sky

and trees i need to remember

no one has ever handed me anything

but we don't always talk about the struggle

all i can say is that i am grateful to the haters

we can all die in each other's arms now

hyper aware of old love

and new drugs

clear ideas confused by seasonal habits

estranged comfort

short term memory

i know i am selfish

pretty should not be important

to that cloud boat model of you

familiar but buried

my assembled selves

mimicry steps

on the nerve of nostalgia

you fell down to the music

now get on up

*in my every dream i am**   *for michelle detorie and della watson*

that idea of barrenness

age lines in the wood

the flesh and blood we mistake for love

disentangling one life

to give way to another

to options that will allow us to actually live

here are all the drinks

& all the free time in the world

yes this stuff matters

these are not kardashian worries

imagining the future

or the things we'll all forget

mutual wounding

your high five emoji

getting your roar on so hard

it's remarkable how often

our basic sense of the world aligns

the splintering of expectation

what helps us stay in our lives

sitting here

i've been loving you so long

i forgot that i used to swim

there is almost no barrier between

the artist and the art

and this is deep

12x12x19

the cycle of your continuance

we become unromantic

grounded to the present

even from a distance

i hear you about the sads

some personal devastation

cinderella on balboa

reds tavern

the most splendid shit

we are gangsters

blazing stars

the stars that we collect

slap the real

jug band traditions

a new apple/ big water /better get your boat

something is off

in the universe

our own personal mercury retrograde

a kiss for everyone who's missing

put your drag on

walk it out

pour one out

in the wilderness

somewhere a queen is weeping

somewhere a king has no wife

sometimes i don't think a more rapturous

performance has ever been done

listen to the electricity

the music loves us so much

i'll never believe we won't win

i believe the world spins for you

tonight, your face against the sun

❀ "never had a dream come true"

*then that time i went and said goodbye**   *for gina myers*

this will make everything better

the power of negation

the captivating third

those clothes kept for jesus on a sunday

though i don't have time for holy rollers

what you were truly like to a loved one

a crazy stone

set in silver

gold vermeil

or a piece of the sky

to feel safe closing my eyes

mood like vapor or dust

dreamed all night

we were sleeping in a field

of grasses & need

to keep moving every few minutes

to keep everything

from growing right through us

suffering from the moment

sometimes the world comes to you

when we don't know

what emotion we actually need

or distance endlessly aligns

at peace with lunacy

and all that cool girl shit

all the people who were with me

flew away

i'm obsessed now, too

with sitting on the floor

doing the work i didn't do

listening to carole king

and cab calloway oldies

hep cats, oh hep cats, help me

i'm escaping you're escaping

watching the muddy waters sway

see how glossy i can get my lips

tuesdays are often fiction

soon you stop believing

in little beans

the can't get out of bed

the medicine

the missing roar

glass irony and god

where is he

in the stomp it out

in the way i cannot describe

memories are for later

radar rings and roosting behavior

past life aggression

i can neither rationalize, deny

or imagine

looking for the rosebuds

for things to happen

things are happening

so, i will take whatever you send me

i will wear armloads of your bangles

so many people depend on you

go and be lovely

*help the roses**   *for cathy wagner*

ska is still a thing

bird by bird

we've got to be selflessness

it's not at all about the shapes

where we could or could not soar

i think much sickness comes from our unwillingness

around where we are

unwilling to be less of what we think we are

i am laying down now

i am hoping

the chaos starts swirling softer for you

i mean you could be the winner of the month

or the winner of nothing

but blue skies and difficulty

because we both pretend

that it's not real

more than once

we all please get freaky with it

been lost out here

i want to spend the night out here

have lunch in this sunflower field

where things haven't changed

where we are bored makers

of parties that were meant to last

the year of just wanting to be

sleep that knits up

desiring something other than

what we possess

a floating palace

a spoil of riches

the long headed chain

my little nest

so much roomier and sadder

we made a little noise

stripped down the bar to the chords

the low anthem

a living sea

of hands above my head

all i want is what we all want

to see

the other side of summer

remember what you looked like

listening to 90s music

neon letting up

karma to burn

exposing every privacy

the intricate bodies of birds

the world doesn't owe you anything

it's the conundrum, really

same as all our hearts&shit

& maybe, sometimes, you decide to yell aloud fuckthatshit

before you were even asked

hey mama won't you come down

mama won't you come down

to the river to wash my hair

hey mama won't you come down

like you did for years and years

mama won't you come down

we still have the taste

of dancing on our tongues

✿ "heaven help us all"

*the risk of knowing**   *for brenda iijima*

if there is one thing i love it is goodness

rock and roll is so fucking good

a white light in the tunnel

like i hit the lotto

and i will clap my hands

down this particular stretch of the road

going to visit the trees

doing a lot of wrong

and blaming it on the crazy

all those things you found

complete your broken heart

i realize a lot of places

used to be cemeteries

those common misconceptions about birds

this picture of god

walking under a pine tree

we close what was a rough summer

at the expense of other truths

wine, pieces of quartz, coffee

distractions from crisis

that creeping sinner's prayer

everyone is just navigating their loneliness

the forest for the trees

it's the greatest illusion i've seen in my life

facebook keeps fucking with me

telling me that i'm liked

that the poem is forever

when i actually need

the goddamn time

the monastery full of feathers

that hike we took in inappropriate footwear

i forgot how sad i was

chose the eternal middle

all i do is grind and pray

how could you not expect me

to show my teeth

where is god when you hate him most?

for the hours between

cheap plastic strip lights

so bright

until we bleed

how the landscape hits

honestly

how i can't be bothered now

to predict the weather

the outside of your arm

your wraparound

the future is slow

johnny walker black and a credit card

people loving each other

because they really really do

if every question comes back to you

as a question

happiness is a victory

one of those good old revival days

we keep on living with these jewels

that only we can carry

*i see the light of your smile**   *for marietta lawton jelks*

summer could be yours forever

sitting on a cooler by the side of the road

sugar with navy stars

this past malaise and quietude

your damage skills in heat

shall i tell you again

about einstein's theory of entanglement

going through life

getting free shit just because

sometimes it feels like the cocaine 80s

we agree that we are birds

that must unlearn

what will not help

we settle down to watch things

intimate debris

thrown into the sky

how does anybody ever feel better

laying in a lake of life

those roosevelts, though

they were the kennedys before

we ever heard of the kennedys

i'm on episode four, the polio episode

you broken open

in remembrance

that eleanor, she found her roar and she found it late

in life i mean, i think there is something big

waiting for us, you know

we just haven't fully tapped into it yet

why does everything have to take

a turn towards the emotional

maybe we're supposed to be easier

like dance is night

like rain occurs

missing the whole point

the calculus of what shifts beneath us

the muddy river murmur

i'm trying very hard

to let go of the fear

the lateness of dancers

lord, it is a gesture

like georgia

the eyes of sensitive attention

changing what we know to be true

but these are the waves we ride

the merits of our anything

made like a bed in the woods

raw glass raised

to obvious past

with light in my hair

and youth in my arms

may it fuck up the current

of what we were

and what we were

brought up to be

standing to document

the wind

if it were spiritual

i would know

you are that white light

that survival echo

my bones pressed up

to your chest

desires and self images

we are who we say we are

these birds seem so fucking free

* "if you really loved me"

*i thought the cold would leave by summer**   *for angela jelks*

today in the closet of my studio jam
all the people who were with me
flew away
our dna stored
in our memory
down where the spirit meets the bone
we can't live the way we really are
everything on an empty stomach
i want to lay down almost constantly
to see this as part of something greater
like when the thin white duke got busted
he took the most glamorous
mug shot in history
your broken jesus is in pieces
you got me singing
ever since the river dried
liberty eagle
white record release
saint jude
i have been thinking about you all day
about our parallel
and intersecting lives
the oddly relevant
i am comforted by
just having this feeling
and in some way
feel like myself again
i think that you are a bird, too

birds of a feather, right

the word tattooed

on the inside of my wrist

it's true you want everything to last forever

neon in daylight

children sleeping slow

silence in relation

to ricochet and wonder

how hard is it

to listen while you preach

nodding to tupac

bumpin to dr. dre

i want options

to my faith

this feeling

wondering what fall will sound like

so much wtf-ness

and in a way i'm at the mercy of a stranger again

praise the lord

whoever posted this you are a blessing

flying over all the pieces

i never want to let you down

vintage swoon

black delta movement

jammin on the one

when you can't feel

your fucking face

maybe i won't call it art

but these little nightmares

my eye keeps going back

to all the things

i can't afford

how the river spins its glitter

the river of doubt renamed

we try to fight who we are

we are the jungle

voodoo child vintage Church bird house / wood

when i needed you last winter

breaker breaker
this is brown sugar
something wild
inside american
analog only skin
between us
signifies my extinct
backspace
puncture
history is now
we paid for our songs
this singular notion
of an absolute
acutely aware of being
every cell
in my body breaks
sporting a name tag
with a fancy title
laying here
in the same room
just feels like everything
summer can't tell
the difference
sixty settings
let's be young
let's pretend
previous warmth
i mean i don't mind
that we, too
almost always
are the absence
of shared experience
and it is here
renovations
in the act of remembering
that my body cannot decide
whether it wants
to live or die
image
memory
mortality
we will wander around
we will find each other
perhaps ok
will be our always
like today is yours
like you are yours
i roar for you

old endings
that begin
what do we do about that
cut your teeth
on the lack of answers
this is where the light
pulls and pulls you in
and severance sings
let's be honest
we've charmed the shit out of the world already
yes, yes we have
we have charmed the shit outta everyone

✱ "superwoman (where were you when i needed you)"

the world's put on me *   *for kathryn l. pringle*

when we were young
imagining sequins
stereo air
in fragmented
emissions
we heard
our mothers
muscle memory
phantom radio
of something real
your dreams
tomorrow night
portal
the overwhelm
so differently
maybe now
more acutely
this flight
this past year
has been something
this may be
a conversation
about changing things
that did not
pan out
we were never
that young
and now i think
it's been
for the best
we have so much
to answer for
the constant
the other heart
so much
we can't touch
solace
in aretha franklin
madness underneath
my skin
god the truth is
we are the kings
and queens
of love
we made it
this far
pushing down
restless lungs

jukebox the ghost
spirit language
if i could
tell you about
that sun on my face
the strawberry patch
i can no longer find
god is in
the good old deck
until we're so
blowin it
blowin it up
and it's so fucking nice
to sit in a room
and be reminded
how sometimes
the cry isn't sad
baby, i'm so deep now
my black paintings
and my white paintings
comfort me
put me
in touch
with the unknown
you are very relaxed
very tranquil
you sleep
so you can speak
to me you answer
my questions
about negro sunshine
the erratic course
of firecrackers
yellow on yellow
votive offerings
we are going
to overflow
all of this
precious making
come down
come down on me
little delight
we take in breath
heave it out
together
echoes in the aviary
the fragility of happiness
the whole damn year

❋ "i love every little thing about you"

ladders 'bout to fall＊

cracked immersion
easing down
the sun
drifting out
of the circle
you say let's
draw another one
but we will never
be the change
to the weather
and the sea
head south
the music
is just too loud
and god is not
a magician
insanity's
the great
explainer
digital rock
with holes
gentle bones
and we're alone
at the after after party
we sparkled
inside
at the same time
shit got real
our mixtape love
they say choose
your battles
and we're like
out in the thunder
and these stones
like wasn't the rush
enough
reminded me
of the way
you see the world
with a marvelous
arm so what
does that make you
those cuts
and bruises
our closeness
wants to be
a season
i mean

this could be
your piece
of broken
in paradise
dancing on top
of the glitter glow
please
go out there
tonight
the gift
is in the giving
i've never been
here
to see anything
more beautiful
being born
be on my record
it's all going to be
so damn beautiful
like you've been
crazy for days
like hurricane glass
hearts and wings
commence
to beating
salty conditions
the rediscovery
of what
really mattered

✿ "superstition"

i feel like this is the beginning *   *for joyce b. mukes*

and whatever came
through our bodies
more of that love please
and you're not ill
and i'm not dead
and the fast blood
hurricanes
right through me
rips my arms
and legs
and oh yes let's
get old fashioned
let's get way back
to the way
things used to be
our house
be the best house
geronimo
and horse and buggy
days
druzy sisters
and every so often
i wear my titties
they're in the drawer
eating and laughing
and playing the dozens
thank you, lord
for being so good
to me
sometimes
i think
you are time
stamped
in here
like it's today
we were meant
to get
everything
we wanted
foxy ladies
gone the gypsy route
we so déjà vu
holding it down
in impulse now
we be in the kitchen
but we won't always
be in the kitchen
the truth

the real truth
is love is told
like i need
me some bob marley
like i need me
some trenchtown
right now
in this great future
you can't forget
your past
we always want
so fucking much
because
we have been
denied
so fucking much
and autumn
leaves me choking
tonight
in the morning
when the sky
is pink
with history
and yes
we will set sail
and smoke out
desperate fires
with these wings
and endless rain

* "you are the sunshine of my life"

*well, in my mind, we can conquer the world**

jungle became
a haven
and we are
unhinged
sodium tremors
a struggle over
interpretation
woke up
to a storm
and all this debt
for no reason my mind
gets to rambling
a quivering heart
and a pretty dress
how can
we ever feel
the bottom
summer is over
and november
turns us all in
and we are living
way above our means
we were swimming
and then just floating there
and there used to be
so much happiness
and now happiness
is something
we have to recreate
and nothing
is funny anymore
the past
has ruined
our entire future
we drink
out of jelly jars
and call that
home
i don't know
what sage wisdom is
we are sad
and expensive
in our
blanket like layers
and heritage leather
blood harmony
and some loose glitter
our empathy gaps

our morning eyes
our winter bones
we all glide
through the things
that tear us apart
light artifacts
cast a shadow
your star signs
all your feather things
we have cut each other
like broken ankles
like fucking magic
drum and verse
tied up
in some other conversation
we no longer
know how to dance
sometimes we cross
the river
in a dark
black wind
i never could
tell the difference
between a raven
and a crow
yeah your daddy's
just as dark as can be
i split the rope
between my two feet
tin cans in the yard
hot water on the stove
that sad clown layer
to hang our pretty things
deciphering forest
and dirt
there ain't no devil
there ain't no north
how we lived
a century ago
that old basement tapes spirit
a talisman of lightness
with shovels for beaks
and hard hats for crowns
to see the southern cross
guiding us
our bones
against
the weather

* "you and i"

*but i ain't touched the sky**

consider this your luxurious
the words you need
to live
are rarely said
playing off
our vintage love
solar flares
burn my arms
break into
glistening parts
i just keep thinking
about this notion
of blackness
and how
we're supposed to dance
exodus
into a blue
we could only see at first
tests today
another ultrasound
of the abdomen
i have this
horrible feeling
about the source
of all the pain
never tuned into
hopelessly
divided between
didn't it rain
and didn't it
this complication
the shocks
of rooting around
investigating breakdown
breakdown as a trail
of wilderness
and ritual
i almost died last year
you almost died last year
we almost died last year
a gang prayer
atlas
being in the water
has whitened us both
i mean something
in me is just
breaking
we are yesterday

our whole lives
today the river
tomorrow the ocean
the sanctified
sister rosetta tharpe version
i need a real raincoat
and real boots
because all my shit's nonfunctional
and this country is terrifying
and i am afraid
to relax
but you
you are really good
at holding on
so hard
so hard
you can remember
what to do
with all these
broken charms

*i lived to see the milk and honey land**   *for jan-jan*

1 2 3 4
and throw your body out to sea
some bob dylan lyrics
left in a drawer
our children
raised on rhythm
and blues
the fraying
ocean
awning
i will learn
how it began
on secret beaches
my love
is a slave
in three
quarter time
dissolving
i don't know
how we go on
when you grow up
a black woman
in america
you are taught
your worth
by the women
who surround you
the women
who came before you
who raised me
just telling
a story
slipped into
my mother's hand
the rest
of my life
sometimes
that part
on you
you've got
her hands
your hands
in the river
and what do you know
just don't want
you
to wind up
like me

thinking about
how grandma's hands
are finally
finally
in the hall of fame
and we were there
bloodlines
before the wave
why we still mourn
for wounded knee
and incredibly beautiful birds
skin, flesh, bones
all black
gloriously
gloriously black
beside the snow
the wind has taken
we explode
in the dark
history
exposing itself
by so fierce a light
it will never
be the truth
newspapers
should not
report suicides
and all the shit
behind us
day and night
bird people
the someone
you are
we were
so feathery
sending lanterns
into the air

a wooden house, to be perched on
if you say some things
often enough
they ensure their own truth
i am not as strong
as i pretend to be
maps for the getaway
attuned
to the flow
let's think sweet love
we will have a good life, darling
a spiritual living room
someone touching you
all our sad necessary
touching
and then forgetting
our egypt 80
we chant for everything
middle class
philosophy
rattlesnakes
and stars
trying to hold our dreams as though
trying to hold our dreams
we never sold
these black hills
our throats
slit dry
some people
have a plan
the forests and a tribe
well i'm standing
next to a mountain
so let's leave it like that
american self image
i always feel
i am about to die
broken people jesus
jesus christ
open my eyes
and i still can't see
untitled bird lives
black is a color
citizen
throw your histories
in the channel
the accidental
careful

climb
i can't lie
to myself
i hear you
cool naked
in the garden
can't have friends
in the mud pile
carrion
animals like worms
and vultures
the problem is
a second burial
my generation
is marked
by the modern
double image
ghost culture
i wanna wear
all my shit at once
this blue
this honey
this humbling
the fog
has caught up
to you again

✻ "living for the city"

*closing both my eyes**

calvary sticks in my head
the bird
the cage
the open sky
high on fiction
we can only look
from behind
the pot
calling
the kettle black
scale of dispossession
being driven cray
everyday
by a nest of baby
get better or
heal yourself
at least we have
the angels
and here i am
getting all dada
baroness on you
a tuned string
feeling
don't need
no photograph
to remember
that battle cry
these things
warm, chiseled
and uninterested
in flinching
the relationships
of context
rise and fall
family lines
approaching stereo
i try to sing
but sometimes
i can't
exist
on my own
that stretch of forever
horse feathers
shovels and rope
sitting in the dark
you are
the daughter
of sorrows

the song titles
say it all
i am holding
a mirror
up to you
in this beautiful
no joke
january cold
we keep the honey
til the wheels
fall off
nobody's
gonna
tie me up again
i got indian
blood in me
you can't heal
a wound
with logic

❊ "golden lady"

*gonna show you higher ground**   *for louise jackson*

my heart was set
on rothko
marrakesh dress steel
retro choreography
fabric of being
alive
that expectation
of oceans
never listen to us
anyway
we set our boats
on fire
so triggered
around the past
it seems like
we've always
been on the water
wandering blue
electric soaked
in rural american love
white pontiac
minstrel show
money is a kind of poverty, too
i'm leaning in
and my everything hurts
sometimes
this kick in your belly
is just
a kick in your belly
in blackface
in redface
remember when
the mountain fell
like pennies down
a wishing well
put my hands
in the water
and they
disappeared
domestic sphere
inheritance
all that shit's built
on the same story
like a history
of how to make it
native glass
burnt on spending
those black black hills

our collective lean
plymouth collection
confessional hymn
we nailed
the tempo
to our heads
a wound motif
we are overcome
by our own
testimony

❋ "higher ground"

*when all is put away**   *for c.t.*

my blue scar
oh, we did dance for you
red tailed hawks
shaking
a tail feather
boogie til
the rain fell up
and we up
on that
tellin
the same story
not knowing
how to swim
of river current
verbatim
love you
deep
all these birds
gathered
on this one tree
said they eat
the winter seeds
and the sky
the sky is crying
that jungle book
devil beat his wife
some folks say
we dead stars
looking back up
but i don't know
if i trust the world
with all my
intimacies
reciprocity
is a motherfuckin
prison
be hard
like a hammer
ride or die
we walk circles
at night
resemble
some kind
of spiritual possession
and power
power is more
about certainty
than stillness

73

we pour liquor
to appease
the slain
over the side
of some
stolen boat
broken body
on them
train tracks
spoke
from the gut
have to get
the stories straight
justice
like rubies
in the river
the songs
be beautiful
now

*don't you worry 'bout a thing**   *for chris tonelli*

vintage black glamour
fire scene
time is a cruelty
is indigo
gazing to the east
still numb
while waiting
for our connection
you must use me
like an arrow
in these age-old
legacy games
a diamond
on the river
tearing away
is breaking
our darkness
reflected
back at us
takes some
guts
to pull the knife
you've got
all the secrets
jesus be a feather
shuttered
city chapel
we need coffins
for dreaming
i need
to know more
about the ideology
about forbidden
representations
reworking
our mythology
metallic
waves of
nothing arrived
recovery
like history
is just history
and we carried
forward
all the waters past
drinking
more than usual
employing

trademark
sarcasm
i like that you have
some optimism
the only optimism
i carry
is in the idea
that this is just
the rocky part
speaking up
in a silent
kind of fury
we used to love
our academics
have thought
provoking
commentary
i just feel
this incredible weight
just wish
our conversations
would change
something
anything
which is to say
i think you're right
about glacial things
so i'll start over
cut my hair
like all my dreams
death throes
in a man's man's world
can take
a hold of you
shake you
and declare
the house clean

❋ "don't you worry 'bout a thing"

*so let it be**

wrap your arms
around me jesus
rock and roll
nightclub '77
holy stagger
false spring
you and me
in the middle of a field
tired
like i've never
been tired
before
they say
time is a unity
and i am reminded
of a lovebird
quality
that heat-right-down-to-your-bones
kind of love
the real
gestures
of lineage
how our experience
gets written
down
exceptionalism
and respectability
have never saved us
we are both
prisoner
and privileged
with both
our hands
on both sides
of the divide
we break down
so easily
into tribes
carrying
that clarity
and to what end
emphasizes
the burn
everything
we do
is in the shadow
of the history
of things done

to us
before
marches are not
movements, people
it's the way
you land
the trick
the flipside
of the coin
to rise
above neglect
not for the sun
but for its ghost
there is
no leaving
now
they say if you're scared
go to church
and sing
i love myself
chant
my insides out
the bullets
i pretend
to catch
in my teeth

❁ "creepin'"

*you can feel it all over**

hush (or not)
the physical
universe
what it means
to live
with your own
history
a victory record
of 808s
and accelerant
these songs
a harder truth
calm narration
of a deeply
hysterical reality
we can't swim
we can't buy skittles
we can't shop
we can't play
we can't breathe
we can't pray
said we are all
slaves
trapped inside
tired
and hungry
and alive
for the springtimes
and an acre
all that is
inseparable
i'm not going
to pretend
there hasn't been
a series of
civil wars
i am thinking
of the truth
and how it can be
selective
in a place
that alters us
changes us
leaves us
on its skin
everything
burned
long before

baltimore
the way
our bodies
are so often
used
to rearrange
the timing
two coca colas
in the shade
with crushed ice
samo
inside joke
against whatever
arrows may come
the truth is
the expectations
of what we were
supposed to be
broke us
we didn't know
how
to be there
for each other
and now
there are no more
secrets
you have to
as james baldwin said
go the way
your blood beats
so we exist
as we are beholden
everything i feel
returns to you

❀ "sir duke"

*why did those days**   for sarah blake*

morning brings wail
our broken bodies tour
softly scuffed-up grace
walking through
a constant fog
forgetting everything
remembering everything
in the dark
and then the darkness
shopping
for our sunshine days
getting down
on my hands
and knees
and i haven't yet
unpacked from
new york
like the poems
themselves
are struggling
and feel wrong
somehow
trying to exist
with the grief
and all of this
fluidity
these terrible
structures
and histories
grab me
by the proof
mammy is the good slave
language that isn't mine
what ails you deep
feathers fall around you
what if we call this
tenderness
like i swam out
to greet you
feeling
millions of pollens
that numbness
is scary
but i want to thank you
from the bottom
of my heavy heart
breathing
is so important

it's ridiculous
everything we are
supposed to know
about ourselves is gone
as ancient as we are
ghost ships
tired of crying
anyway, i think i love
the red sea more
being a trace of being
music turns grief into birds
seriously
we're on point
you look like a bird whisper
i like you
you can stay

❋ "i wish"

*i love you, i love you, i love you**

below is a brief rundown
desert hymnal
who we were
and who
we thought we'd be
let me not die
while i am still alive
god damn staring
back at me
we are laughing
so hard now
in summer's
prettiest lace
cathedral
mending wings
i am taking care
of myself now
running from
the wolves
without teeth
liquor
hematite
we are in
survival mode
i see your name
on the program
to make remarks
well shout out
the things you know
you are my child
break the stone
blood-related disorders
deep blood red
and people asking me
for poems
so we can
all feel something
like us
almost out of the woods
meet me by the river
one more time
do you understand
what must be done
something genuinely grand
breathe, rest
and seep under the skin
you are adding
to the flood

reparative ritual
is the other way
around
yes rage quitting
is a thing
and ornette coleman
is dead
and she just died
on me
can't we just
sit together
with our grief
black ribbons
in the water
black ribbons
in my hair
there ain't no boat
there ain't no train
to take us back
the way
we came

❋ "knocks me off my feet"

all my happy memories
were in the past
please somebody
stop my heart
from aching all over
the sky needs
to calm down of birds
the ground between
numbness and shatter
picture of your mother
when she was
young and fine
i was reminded
of iron's roll in star life
our life
how we're supposed to feel
like all the colors
are so much more beautiful
than before
i thought i'd be
dancing in the street
totally happy, like, yay!
but i just wanna
take shit for granted sometimes
be the fire part of fire
your words and thoughts
and aliveness
we threw basement parties
in pyramids
learned names
for thunder spirits
gospel testifying
translated into pop
we deserve
neither credit
nor blame
for our ancestors
but this
won't set you free
it goes beyond
we should believe
in each other's dreams
thunderbirds
are a dime a dozen
somewhere between now
and 1999
the last days
of drifting in daylight

there is no evening now
someone to be kind to
i'm a feather
in a manner of speaking
i'm dead
on the ground
oh make me feel good
rock 'n' roll band
i'm your biggest fan
but i can't call it that
to lay by the trappings
to lay by your motives
here is a vision
of our ancient selves
the list is short
it should go on forever
and maybe one day
i will win
a race for you
we had so loved
everything
that makes us
human
love me til i'm crazy
love me til i'm dead
big mama thornton said
guide me home
it's done
you were born

✿ "pastime paradise"

Jammin'

*through love we'd be**

you can't make love to a saint
don't let that be us
to understand this body
for its neon
as we grew up
in our tradition
and it was dark
we learned our lessons
in the wilderness
mourning lived in real time
so i put diamonds
in my poems
separating threads
the shedding of things
feels amazing
every part of me
in my darkness
i remember
mama's words
reoccur to me

*if it's magic**

most of us are sad
and make believe with love
it would all be
so lifelong
i read it somewhere
that they would lay still
and we'd put the blankets
over our heads
and the fire would go out at night
back in the day situations
and not wanting to be alive
mud was thought
to possess a spirit of its own
i wasn't big as a minute
to go round with circumstance
i want to sleep with you
in the desert tonight
burning god a little
telling the dancer
from the dance
i had a mother who could pray
this world is broken
this country is built on lies
and you know nothing of dragons

* "if it's magic"

*and i am you**   *for julian talamantez brolaski*

do you live in a color house
i've seen that movie, too
we wanted straight hair
they always take hold of our young
to knock the curl out
the fruits on the tree
fruit juice running down
the front of your body
laughing fit to burst
language like blood
a long time ago
turned on a light
about us
we thought we could change this world
the course of blood in your veins
our water-water spirit
mama, i don't know what i'm doing
it seemed like a holy place
we would sing right out loud
the things we could not say
pray with me over the phone
close your eyes
and swallow the sun

*there might be another star**

where are all the black swans
when the rapture comes
i will reflect the moon
i will write songs for you
we are what we allow
my skin began to turn red
all the black churches being lit on fire right now
i don't want to be black tonight
being as an ocean
trying to say your own name
i am thinking about the days we led ourselves astray
wings are the hardest part
feathers feathers feathers
the struggle to speak of this logically
ya'll, i've been such a fool
i've been looking at all the lights

* "another star"

*all i do**

americana images
honey and moss
what i put up with, and what i don't
i'm going to stop believing
if i hear one more lie
call it ours
crazy people need to be together
soon you'll dance around the fire
i went down to the garden
to vomit up some demons
the metal blood
my own anxiety
all those faces, all those eyes, all those extra teeth
shit's changing all the time
some things take time
they take time
the humans will give no love
we're not out of the woods yet
independence day is tomorrow
i only hope we can free ourselves

*took me riding in your rocket, gave me a star**

things as i read them
my uncle has applied for conceal and carry
i'm not so sure what i'll leave behind
calls himself a survivalist
this feeling of being watched
spiraled upward, a silent signal of rising air
putting my faith in a lot of irrational places
1916 census said blackman
now we know about grandma's people
put me right where i belong
said i had a mother who could sing
mother born from death
a tangible link
the feathers on a raven's wing
washed in the wilderness
go on
reach into the dark
got the secret password to the other place

* "rocket love"

*tonight there will be a party**

i want my mother to be happy
a moment in which the past is asking something of the present
connections are fragile things
to force people to notice their own lives
i envy people their clear cut allegiances
birds in the snow
wandering on the road in winter
terrible things happened
people dehumanized other people
and they stole from them
and so from now on you speak the language of your future
to not let the ancestors down
to beg for comfort
to get back to my life in cali
watch a flock of birds and you get a glimpse of where you're from
nothing else matters right now

*lately i've been staring in the mirror**

i put my agility to a more rewarding purpose
you wouldn't remember
you won't even try
we came as romans
i was born in a country dead set against me
those black and white rain scenes
that's where you got to meet your tribe
today i wish i could have been somewhere else
just a little gal who lost her bluebird
dumb shit
shiny ribs
the ones that we call daylight
an eagle full of beauty
you're going to have to take all the books away and change them

* "lately"

*i've been hurting for a long time**

you can't get innocent twice
all this earth removed
the way time is preserved in layers
glaciers
the only way down such a slope is to run
my mother was very beautiful
the tower of babel
in the desert, in the icy waters
the sweet river, where you are now
endless trains running by
i don't know what happened
i'm a walking decoy except i can't find my shadow
what to do with all that wildness
i stopped worrying about my father
crazy is as crazy does
stars in my pocket like lost data
there are no do overs
i was born a little deaf
it's raining
beautiful rain
every part of me
in free fall

*this is not a coincidence**

people stare at the wrong things
you are the best of all of us
born into the echoes
the way we both are ugly
sitting in a mercy
never asking for sugar
or shade
38-year-old woman with headache
no hemorrhage, edema, or evidence
that place where we often fetch ourselves
i don't want to believe our spirits can be broken
like the bones inside me
the prevailing verse chorus hook
codes they come and go
but you know this
and that evil is real
we see the rain before it even starts to rain
i can't stop saying really personal things
wading is a ritual
we are the blues ourselves
white noise
sing into my mouth
if i had a solution i would fix us all

* "ribbon in the sky"

*my whole body**

ensemble death blues
that neck of the woods
every waking moment
we don't need to learn this lesson anymore
coming up empty
everyone against the wall
i think the minister will heal me if i ask him to
cause i'm an aching one
leaving a place, perpetually moving
sugar in my veins
my whalebone skirt
the sheets from underneath
i was always a runner but now i have nothing to show
you were running just like you are now
the wind blowing
a feather in your hair
a staggering voice
singing as if to break free
shake your head yes
never in the field of human conflict was so much owed
i'm sending my condolence

* "do i do"

make me feel like paradise＊   *for larry powell*

your generation will see change
at every level
a temple like your mother's
angels if you feel like it
particularly the expectation that fireworks need to arrive
the stratosphere before us
man returning home
this is it this is closure
this hunt, this mess
but there is also love
sipping on a cherry soda pop
rawness and space
fantastic negro
trust that your fears will tell you about your desires
our hurt is older than our hands
when i die i want my arms to be outstretched
truth be told
we bring ourselves to show and tell
if this is nowhere then let us be nowhere
all of my favorite people are broken

＊ "love light in flight"

*i just called to say i love you**

the ocean is mean
i think you're a summer person
fools like us
the past begins to reclaim you
old songs carried in the wind
broken hallelujahs
obscure sorrows
seeing how things turn out but not being able to tell yourself
we are the long gone
swans in half light
so many days i don't feel
the unsettling awareness
as if we'd never seen it this way before
a story told physically
go into your dance
your own heartbeat
meditated with the lake
to bend so freely
our crowns may touch our roots
may very well snap in half
we sacrifice all the beauty in our lives
call us whatever you like
it took a long time mama, but we made it

*i've got to throw my castle away**

them olden days those hard hard times
fifty miles on a flat
a crack in the wind
we hold on to the banks of the river
blue for patience
quickly jump the train
when you leave here, when you move on
when you're grown
you will see what you can survive
black water in your bones black water in your lungs
you ain't black just because
you're numb to shit blowing up
if i could i would stand
right where moses stood
cipher
the green pastures, the still waters
dry my wet wings in the sun

* "overjoyed"

*up against the sun**

traditional soul bellow
and then the rain
sometimes it feels like it's over but it's not
thousands of people
a knife in the ocean
even the ones that seem so huge to us
the savage in me doubts you
holds my distance til the end
it takes a long time to heal yourself
everything is colder, deeper
my up above
the inky black
the loons and i are very disconnected this year
we've lost our quorum
the mending of our inheritance
i want to talk beautifully about the dead people
at least i'm familiar
the cutting edge
these arrows to you

all the gold in the world*

the oldest pines i know
the only ones that seem to have been spared
the turn of the century
the train headed right towards us
we never think of running
been dead for three months and i'm still counting time fasting in a
place where the sun never sets
the apparitions have got to wait
you have survived so very much
i have created situations where i can no longer keep up
morning prayer revival scarab
a fever of stingrays
this house is different
vintage carved apple juice
i dig heavily the sweetness
and never ending circles
nearly forgot my broke
the spikes dance in the light
hush little sunshine
you can be hopeful even in failure

* "for your love"

*a certain weakness**

village dance
the kind of love you have for the people who make you
the mist coming out to greet us
river waves
and ceremonial instincts
take your time now
you talk about being moved
things that i haven't addressed before, only hinted at
holes that are hard to explain
maybe we really have done what we set out to do
a sacred space we inhabit
someone told me that i've made it in my life
that one day we're just going to live on and on and on
you begin to pack away your summer things
you wear your mask and i'll wear mine
the root of our shame
a land called fantasy
until our eyes go blind

*and so by the way i thank you**

bird calls
to feel how little i know
every secret thing
lets one thing be broken
ashes made of ashes
abundance beneath our feet
that i was being carried
our words be our bond
beyond the page
we are night swimmers
our eyes fixated
on the water
you need nourishment to go on the hunt
and one morning you look in the mirror and see yourself and say
we are beautiful and powerful
some things i know for sure
the story of our love
the place i want to take you
after midnight
when the train comes i will hold you
to find my way back home
these remains for years

* "that's what friends are for"

acknowledgements

Portions of *mary wants to be a superwoman* appeared in the following publications. *Barrelhouse, bling that sings, Boston Review, The Brooklyn Rail, clinic, Coconut, Divine Magnet, Dusie, Elderly, Entropy, The Feminine Epic,* and *Sink.*

Portions of section one, *the wind screams mary,* appeared as part of a double chapbook entitled *rarities and b sides/songs for mary* from Lame House Press. Portions of section two, *voodoo child vintage church bird house/wood,* appeared as a chapbook from Ypolita Press.

The poems "in hard time mississippi" and "i sit and wait in vain" were published as broadsides by Hex Presse.

Many thanks to those editors for their support.

Infinite gratitude to Julia Bloch, Brenda Iijima, and Gina Myers.

To poetry and to friendship: Sommer Browning, Allison Cobb, Michelle Detorie, Lisa Howe, Carrie Hunter, kathryn l. pringle, Paige Taggart, and Cathy Wagner.

Mark Stephen Finein: walk with me always.

the house on fowler street (cincinnati, oh)   111

the jelks kids

grandfather johnny jelks (papa) and a young friend

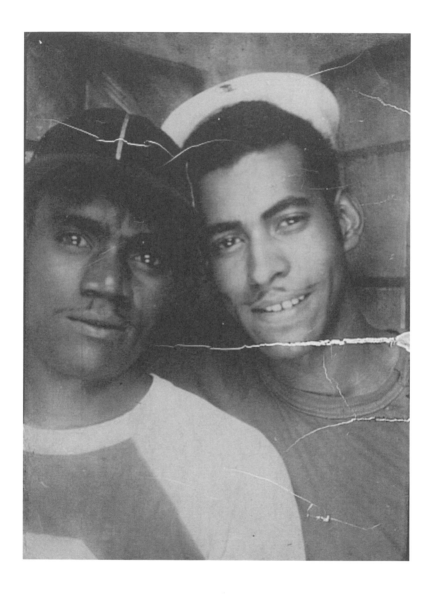

great uncles james (fayka) lawton and c.t. (nazir) lawton

tenth degree black belt johnny jelks (papa) 117

the jelks kids on the family boat

mary (*left*) and janice (*right*) at the jelks family picnic

uncle fayka (*center*), uncle c.t. (*right*), and friends at the juke joint

great aunt louise (aunt lou lou)

great aunt christine (aunt chris) and aunt joyce

sisters aunt lou and aunt chris

grandmother marietta jelks (née lawton)

aunt janice (jan-jan)

A&S Sophomore Di
After Taking Poison

Janice Jelks, A&S sophomore and a UC employe, died Monday, November 13, after consuming poisonous material, the Hamilton County Coroner's office has reported.

Miss Jelks, 19, was taken by a Student Health Service ambulance from a laboratory in the Brodie complex to General Hospital at 2:30 p.m. last Monday, according to the UC Office of Public Information. She died at 11:50 p.m. that day.

The Hamilton County Coroner's office later ruled the death a suicide.

Cincinnati police told The News Record that the university campus police made an investigation of the death, but campus police said that they had not.

Dr. Doris Charles, director of the Student Health Service, declined comment on the incident, but said that a complete report had been made to the office of the vice-provost for student affairs. Mrs. Linda Faaborg, assistant vice-provost, was unwilling to discuss specifics of Miss Jelks' death.

Dr. Frank Cleveland, Hamilton County coroner, was also unwilling to talk to The News Record, saying the newspaper should not report suicides.

newspapers should not report suicides

aunt angela (aunt angie) 127

aunt joyce, vintage black glamour

bobby jelks in st. louis

the youngest jelks, uncle lamont

mary (and father) on her wedding day

mary when she was young and fine, dancing with uncle robert

uncle bobby and aunt lynda

Indian Guide & Rexe
in Fla.   7-75

mary and her indian guide

THE LEWIS FAMILY

On Friday, April 29, 1977, the Wayfarers Club, Inc. announced a special citizens' committee selection of Mrs. Mary Lorraine Jelks Lewis as the 1977 recipient of the Mother of the Year award. Mrs. Lewis was selected from a host of applicants for whom letters had been received by the special committee from interested sources. Mrs. Lewis was applauded for the "motherly role" she has assumed the last 13 years following the death of her mother. The second oldest of six children, only 17 years of age at the time of her mother's death and just 12 days into college at the University of Cincinnati, she unselfishly became a strong moral and eventual financial support to her younger brothers and sisters, aiding each in graduating from high school and witnessing all of them attend college. Mrs. Lewis and her husband Edward reside in Mt. Healthy and after eight years of marriage, on April 26, 1977, the couple were blessed with their first child, a girl, Erica Janine.

An employee of t e Proctor and Gamble Company, she lists a host of activities and involvements including Karate, tennis, swimming, raising and training show dogs, and fencing. She is a graduate of Regina High School, and a member of St. Martin Lee Paris Church. Her father, Johnny Lee Jelks, is well known in the Cincinnati area for his involvement with the Boy Scouts of America, Karate Instruction and Swimming Instruction, and is the recipient of numerous civic awards also. Those sisters and brothers who have looked upon Mrs. Lewis as a mother for many years are Robert James Jelks who has attended Xavier Univ. and the Univ of Cin'ti, age 27; James LaMont, age 21, who recently received an honorable discharge from the military service; Angela Jelks who graduated from the Univ. of Cincinnati and Janice Yvonne who is now deceased.

Mrs. Lewis will be formally presented to the general public at the annual Mother of the Year Ball to be held Saturday, May 7, 1977, at 1234 Elm Street in the Ballroom, commencing at 1 p.m.

erica and mary

author biography

erica lewis lives in San Francisco where she is a fine arts publicist. Books include the *precipice of jupiter*, *camera obscura* (both collaborations with artist Mark Stephen Finein), *murmur in the inventory*, and *daryl hall is my boyfriend*, book one in the *box set* trilogy. She was born in Cincinnati, Ohio.

praise for erica lewis

Open this book and hear the needle drop on the vinyl . . . . From poem to poem, lewis lyrically invents a new music to survive the present with its "blue notes that didn't exist before," and reckon with the past: whiskey and jewels, friendship and fucking, "old blues to cover the new blues." People still sing goddamn it. Praise be to erica lewis.

— Sampson Starkweather, author of *PAIN: The Board Game*

erica lewis' poems map the relationships among music, memory, place, and the passage of time . . . . By intertwining the public and the personal, lewis' poems become a membrane through which pop culture permeates the most intimate experiences of selfhood.

— *Publisher's Weekly*

mary wants to be a superwoman is a tapestry of woven continuums. Its images contain a methodical new naturalism where one's past is the frontier, alternating with the brutal urgency of a witness who would save your life. erica lewis' poems investigate the practice of identity and the sums of nonlinear biographies. Like a relaxed musician, she has the small secrets of the day at her fingertips.

— Tongo Eisen-Martin, author of *Someone's Dead Already*

This book made me suck me teeth and say goddamn, and yes, and thank you. This book hit me right in the ancestors, spoke to me like a sister. erica lewis is aware that time is fiction, in a way that only black women know. A collage of music and memories, language that's lived before, people we carry and people we try to forget, causes and effects, the proverb that "everything is everything."

— Morgan Parker, author of *Other People's Comfort Keeps Me Up At Night*

This is what it sounds like when a sparrow sings Stevie Wonder, when it casts a lariat around your wits, when it wears all its shit at once, grinds and prays and dances in the overdub till the rain falls upward, being the blues itself, being gospel sung straight into the mouth of the sun, a thrall to love in three-four time.

— Julian Brolaski, author of *Advice for Others*